WOMEN ON THE EDGE 2

Ariel Gutraich

maitena

WOMEN ON THE EDGE 2

Translated by Margarita Raimundez
Language Consultants: Mila Maren and Tyrone Merriner

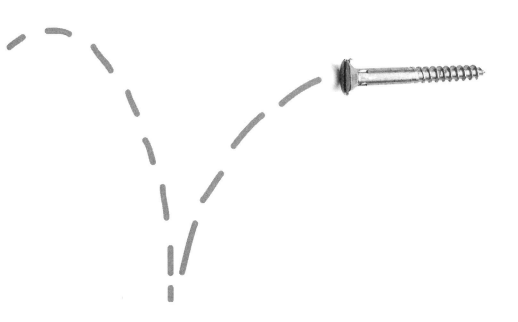

RIVERHEAD BOOKS
NEW YORK

THE BERKLEY PUBLISHING GROUP
Published by the Penguin Group
Penguin Group (USA) Inc.
375 Hudson Street, New York, New York 10014, USA
Penguin Group (Canada), 10 Alcorn Avenue, Toronto, Ontario M4V 3B2, Canada
(a division of Pearson Penguin Canada Inc.)
Penguin Books Ltd., 80 Strand, London WC2R 0RL, England
Penguin Group Ireland, 25 St. Stephen's Green, Dublin 2, Ireland (a division of Penguin Books Ltd.)
Penguin Group (Australia), 250 Camberwell Road, Camberwell, Victoria 3124, Australia
(a division of Pearson Australia Group Pty. Ltd)
Penguin Books India Pvt. Ltd., 11 Community Centre, Panchsheel Park, New Delhi—110 017, India
Penguin Group (NZ), Cnr. Airborne and Rosedale Roads, Albany, Auckland 1310, New Zealand
(a division of Pearson New Zealand Ltd.)
Penguin Books (South Africa) (Pty.) Ltd., 24 Sturdee Avenue, Rosebank, Johannesburg 2196, South Africa

Penguin Books Ltd., Registered Offices: 80 Strand, London WC2R 0RL, England

WOMEN ON THE EDGE 2

PRINTING HISTORY
Previously published in Spanish by Editorial Atlantida S.A., 1994
First Riverhead trade paperback edition: November 2004
Riverhead trade paperback ISBN: 1-59448-094-X

This book has been catalogued with the Library of Congress.

Printed in the United States of America

10 9 8 7 6 5 4 3 2 1

ON THE EDGE, PRIVATELY

Typical ironies in the game of love

Knights in Shining Armor vs. Men

Men are never to blame!

Men like them young

Six simple rules for arguing

A few things men can't understand

When it comes to giving gifts, men fall into six categories

Six things you can't ask a man

Issues that arise when choosing the kid's name

Types of men over forty

Things women say when they don't want to say what's going on

Behavioral differences between divorced men and women

Six secrets to a perfect marriage

ON THE EDGE, ON THE INSIDE

Six ways to know you're motivated by guilt

Six good reasons for being a shallow woman

Signs of spring fever

Are women sexist?

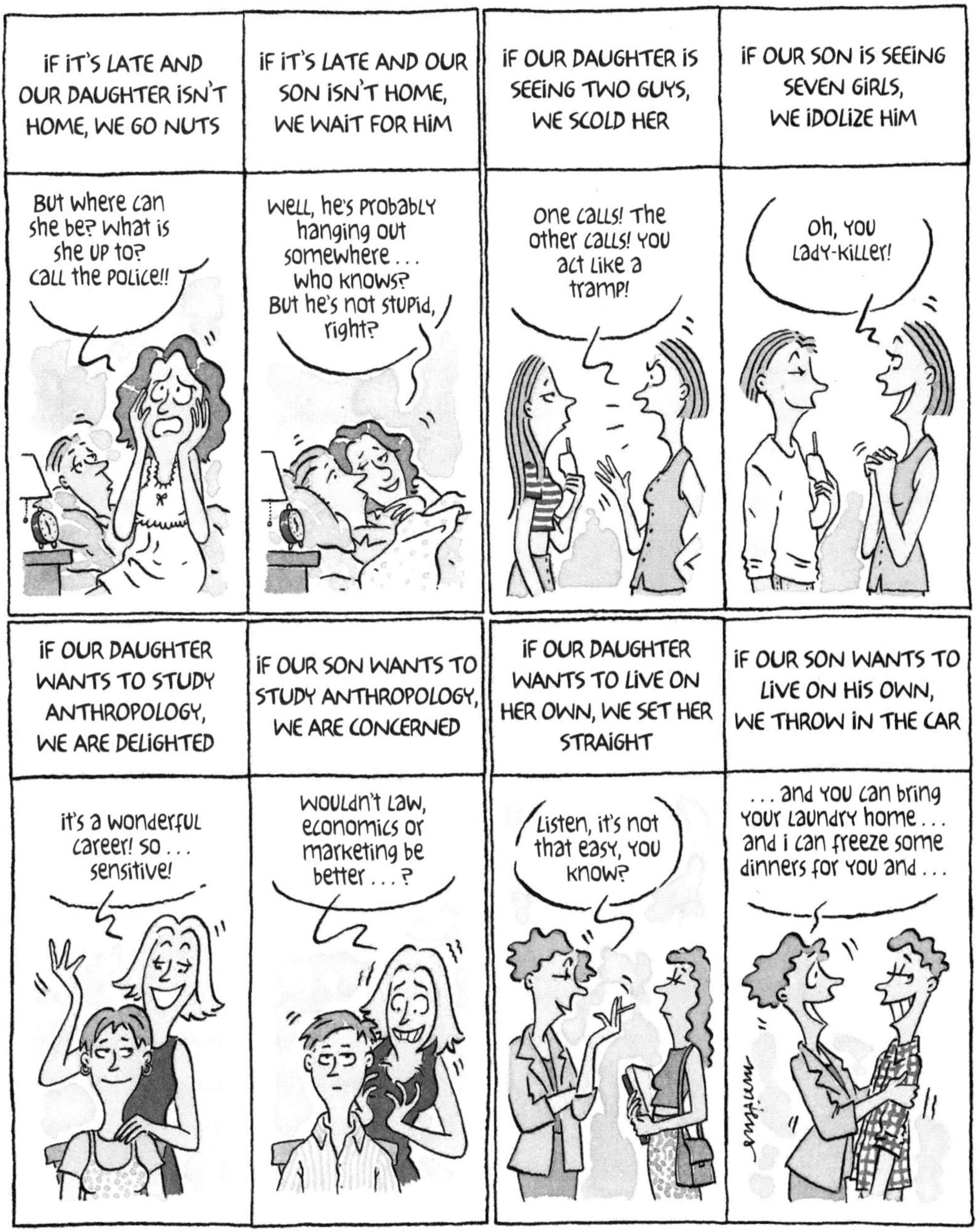

Six classic vacation options

What those of us who resent not taking vacations like to hear from those who did

The despair of waiting for him to call

Six signs you're feeling pretty lousy

Classic moments at the gynecologist

Six reasons to get more depressed on a Saturday night

TWO HUNDRED CHANNELS TO CHOOSE FROM
AND THERE'S NOTHING ON

THE TELEPHONE RINGS,
THE ANSWERING MACHINE PICKS UP . . .
AND THEY HANG UP

YOU RUN OUT OF CIGARETTES
ONCE YOU'VE UNDRESSED

AN ENVELOPE SLIDES IN UNDER THE DOOR:
YOUR RENT BILL

YOUR LAST BOTTLE OF BEER EXPLODES
IN THE FREEZER

YOU GO OUT ONTO THE BALCONY
AND THE NIGHT IS ONE BIG PARTY!

Six good reasons to hate Christmas

ON THE EDGE, PUBLICLY

Great minor tragedies in a woman's life

That strange habit of not seeing ourselves as "older"

Some delightful moments between women and their hair

On women and their inevitable relationship with waxing

The summer responses to dieting

Six potential discoveries when first trying on a swimsuit

The crazy effects of hot weather on fashion

Now playing . . .
our blockbuster hit fashions!

In the good old days, before medical advances . . .

Tell me your age and I'll tell you your doctor

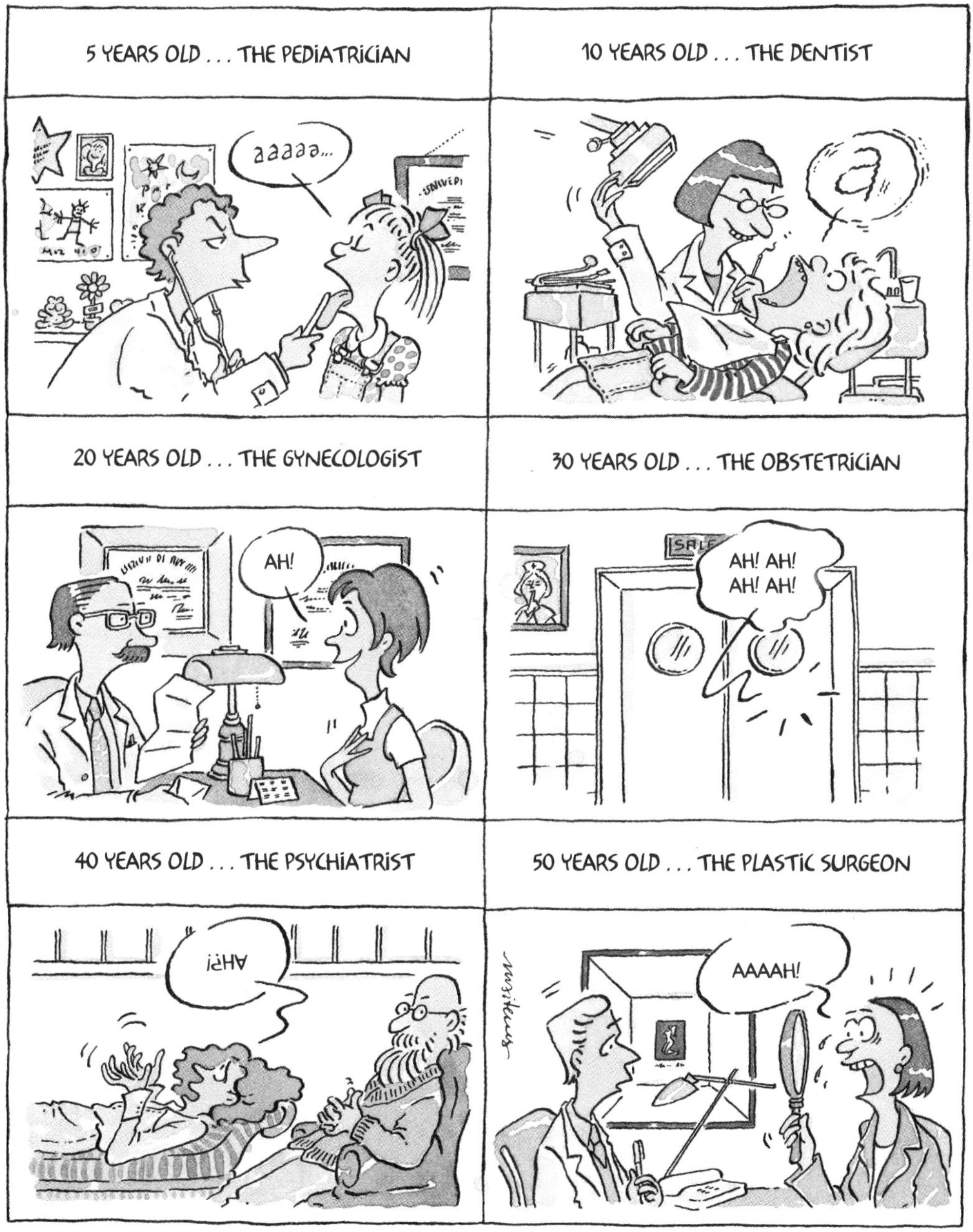

How does a woman define beauty?

ON THE EDGE, DOMESTICALLY

Some delightful things to do the day after the holidays

Tell me your child's age and I'll tell you where *not* to go on vacation

Life is the same at the beach, only you're in a swimsuit

Things we would never have said to our parents

when they said the things we swore we'd never say to our kids

Some of the most common "I don't haves"

Six typical ways women disrupt the game

The Super Bowl!

Kids just love having a dog!

Things have changed in the land of fatherhood

How head lice tempers a mother's character

Six typical back-to-school issues

Stepmothering is a no-win situation

How to turn your son into a sexist male

ON VARIOUS EDGES

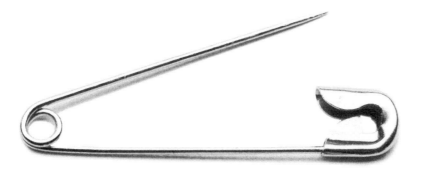

Precious moments with the cordless phone

Answering machine issues

Six good reasons to feel embarrassed for others

Those cheap emotions brought on by sales

The compulsive behavior of horoscope readers

Animals missing from the Chinese zodiac

Friends fall into six categories

Those unforgettable things you forget

Six classic lines when someone wants to dump their kid on you . . .

Great solutions that never pan out

It always rains when . . .

Tell me what you study and I'll tell you what you nag me about . . .

The six worst neighbors on the beach

Six things to expect from those who've just returned from vacation . . .

Unbearable moments, courtesy of a box of matches . . .

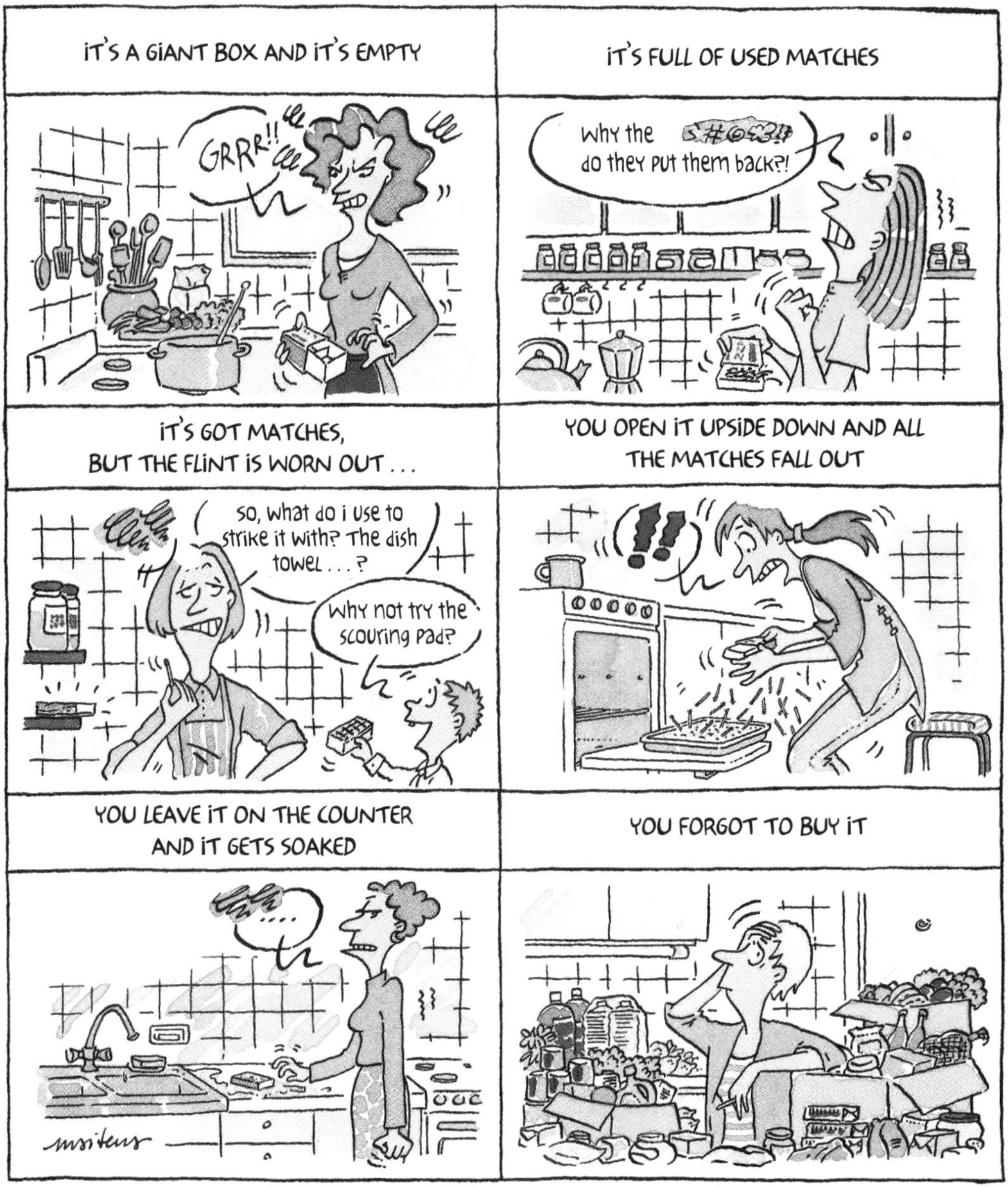

Icy feelings, courtesy of the fridge

TEST

TO MEASURE
HOW CLOSE YOU ARE
TO THE EDGE

We often let out a couple of screams—the kind that makes the building shake—and we immediately feel sorry for what we've done: because we feel guilty, because we'll now have to endure murderous looks from our neighbor in 4B, or because we've hurt our vocal cords on the very day we had choir practice.

Some of us will then sneak down the service elevator, others will apologize, and others will drink a cup of hot milk and honey, laced with six shots of scotch.

All of us will inevitably ask ourselves whether we're . . . on the edge.

Let's set guilt aside. Let's discard excuses, like we inherited our grandmother's temper. Let's avoid running over someone who accuses us of being insane. Let's simply try to get to know ourselves.

Drink a cup of herbal tea and check one answer to each of the questions listed in the following test. Drink a second cup of herbal tea, add up your points and find out how close you are . . . to the edge.

1 You find out your partner is cheating on you.
A: You simply refuse to believe it; he always tells you everything.
B: You talk it over.
C: You burn all his shirts and smash him over the head with a chair.

2 You detect cellulite creeping up your thighs.
A: As it doesn't hurt, you pay no attention.
B: You switch from sunbathing to skiing, from alcohol to mineral water, and from the shrink to the gym.
C: You never leave your house again.

3 You have a problem that keeps you up at night.
A: You discuss it with your landlord.
B: You discuss it with a friend.
C: You discuss it with your dog.

4 You're in a rush and forget your purse in the taxi.
A: You don't notice until three days later.
B: You bawl your eyes out and tell the whole world.
C: You steal the first unattended purse you see.

5 You meet a man who interests you.
A: You forget him five minutes later.
B: You try to seduce him.
C: You ask for his phone number and you call him every fifteen minutes.

6 You agreed to go on a blind date.
A: You forget and stand him up.
B: You show up with a friend.
C: You introduce him to your parents.

7 The hairdresser ruins your hair.
A: You buy a hat.
B: You attempt to murder the hairdresser.
C: You commit suicide.

8 You're invited to the party of your life and you have nothing to wear.
A: You don't go to parties.
B: You borrow something from a friend.
C: You sell the fridge and buy yourself a fabulous outfit.

9 You live alone. It's Saturday night. Your phone's not working.
A: You don't care because the TV still works.
B: You run to a public phone and frantically call everyone to let them know your phone's not working.
C: You move.

10 You're regular. Your period's late.
A: You make an appointment with your gynecologist for the following month.
B: You climb thirteen floors forty-seven times.
C: You laugh.

11 You consult your horoscope in a magazine. The first thing you check is . . .
A: Health.
B: Love.
C: The horoscope of the person you most despise.

12 Your partner tells you to meet him on a corner at a certain time. You're punctual but he's not there.
A: You wait five hours.
B: After waiting half an hour, you call him up and let him have it.
C: You check hospitals and police stations.

13

ou separate and your ex marries one of our friends.
A: As you know what they both like, you send them a beautiful gift.
B: You talk to each of them separately and list all the awful things they don't know about the other.
C: You flirt with her father.

14

ou win a contest. The prize the plastic urgery procedure of your choice.
A: You finally get your hammertoe corrected.
B: Without giving it a second thought, you get yourself a new pair of boobs.
C: You request Joan Rivers's face.

15

You feel lonely. You decide to take up a hobby where you'll meet people.
A: You sign up for an Ikebana course.
B: You register with a political party or an environmental group.
C: You join your local gang.

16

You're walking down a dark street. A man is walking behind you…
A: You ask him what he wants.
B: You look in your purse for your nail file to use as a weapon in case he attacks.
C: Without waiting to find out his intentions, you attack him, scratching and biting the bastard.

17

Your husband remarks that he thinks you've gained a few pounds. You:
A: Absolutely agree with him.
B: Point out his unsightly paunch.
C: Have a fit because he no longer loves you.

18

You've just married when you realize he's very untidy.
A: You apologize for tidying up after him.
B: You tell him to hire a cleaning lady.
C: You ask him for a divorce.

19

Passion has cooled between you and your partner. In order to rekindle it you decide to:
A: Go to the salon for a complete hair removal session.
B: Make him jealous.
C: Ask him if he's gay or just impotent.

20

In the middle of a difficult argument, you run out of words. So, you:
A: Write.
B: Cry.
C: Bite.

21

If you could become a man for a day, what would you do?
A: Shave.
B: Pee standing up.
C: Get into a fistfight.

Now, add up your points.

Each **A** answer is worth **one** point.
Each **B** answer is worth **two** points.
Each **C** answer is worth **three** points.

From 0 to 20 points:

You are not on the edge, you're dead.

From 20 to 30 points:

You tend to deny reality, which, in addition to your growing lack of self-esteem, keeps you reasonably calm. You're close to being on the edge but still not a dangerous person. However, you're not much fun either.

From 30 to 40 points:

You are on the edge, yes, but at an acceptable level for our times. No doubt, if you found the man of your dreams, won the lottery, and shed 14 pounds, you would be all set to face life as happy as a bubble of Champagne.

From 40 to 50 points:

You've got one foot over the edge. Your nervous system dominates all your actions, and not very democratically at that. Take it easy, now . . . try to finish reading without tearing this page out. Consider middle-of-the-road attitudes. You tend not to be for or against anything in particular; you only tend to disagree.

From 50 to 60 points:

You're ready for the straightjacket.

About Maitena